SUBCONSCIOUS MEMORIES

By NEGIN NAMAVARI

SUBCONSCIOUS MEMORIES

Author

Negin Namavari

Illustrator:

Avideh Jahad

DEDICATION

Thank you to all of you for striving to continue and to grow.

Thank you to all the people that have shared their story, whether to me directly or publicized it. Without your voice and courage, so many stories would remain unheard. It is people like you that encourage and help others. Thank you to all the public platforms that strive to give people voices. As knowledge is about having exposure and stories help expose.

No one is alone in what they are going through. Experiences are unique, though there are people that have lived similarly. There are multiple versions of lives people are not aware of, mainly because they have not encountered the people living them. Being able to acknowledge the circumstances of another's life which differs from one's own, can open minds and hearts.

Here is a sample of the lives that surround you.

WARNING:

This book contains stories of explicit detail. It may trigger some individuals and evoke uncomfortable realizations. The following material contains upsetting, uplifting, and diverse perspectives. The purpose is to educate, please continue to read with an open mind.

Not all is recommended for children.

Table Of Contents

The lives not talked about.

CHILD

Blind to how she ended up there
It was just a daily routine
The life she always knew
Not having a single clue
Of the tragedy she was
Going through

Waking up every morning
She brushes her teeth
Grasping her puberty
Counting the change in her pocket
She must give half away
To her only resource and care

She puts on clothes
That will only be removed
As the sun slowly sets
Or sometimes even when it's aloft
She goes to work as the brave
The life of a child sex slave

I SHOULD HAVE ABORTED

I should have aborted
Convinced through guilt
By those who thought they knew best
By a religion unable to be seen
As if God wanted to give this child
A life of aching
From protesters that still want to decide
What I should do with my life
Yet unwilling to help me get by

I had a future
Attaining a degree
Helping those in need
Waiting for stability
Then finding love and having a family
Now taking care of this being
Who will never know half their genes
As I am struggling
Just to provide a beginning

CREATED PURPOSE

So thrilled I kept you
The purpose of life
Amending the ways, I lived life
Giving me a reason to conquer
Unconditional love
Only mother's encounter
Your smile is bliss
My heart has a future
My past was a tutor
Now able to pass it along
The moments spent contemplating
Reassured you are the best thing
To have ever happened to me

MY OWN

A car or a gun
Overdose or jump
Try to make it look like an accident
Or leave a note of remembrance
So many options to end
This toxicity trends
A goodbye to those
That say they care
All I heard was fake
Until the day finally came
I tried to take my own life away

Standing on top of the bridge
Smiling at strangers
Just needing one conversation
To rethink
Nothing of the sort occurs
So, I say one last farewell
As my body falls
Into the deep ocean

There is something about life
Something just beautiful
That before I couldn't have known
Until I tried to take my own
And lived still

FIFTEEN

At the age of fifteen
Thrown out with nowhere to go
Free from the tormenters
Who should have never conceived
With a life of nothing

At the age of sixteen
Foster homes
To friends called druggies
With just one backpack
Being the only property

At the age of seventeen
Deciding to be clean
Living out on the streets
Just to get food without money
While getting a high school degree

At the age of eighteen
Living a secret life
Beneath the tunnels
A temporary home
Trying to make it on my own

At the age of nineteen
Pushing for opportunities
Finally getting work
Education and residency
Just living the beginning

At the age of twenty-three
With a college degree
A life of dreams
Vocal about old secret scenes
Grateful to be out of fifteen

GUILTY URGES

It suddenly came over him
The sexual desires he suppressed
Triggered
Everything around him turning
Pitch black and silent
Feeble torch flickering against only one
As if everything halted
Except his guilty urges
Yearning for respite
Recollection of his own power lost
Determined to regain it
No matter the cost

Driving along
To catch his prey
Rehearsing his script
So, they don't run away
Watching as they play
Predator of the most horrid dismay
He picks as if they were on display
The time to lure arriving
Perhaps one with a familiar face
Reviewing what's been packed
He goes into attack

Now with his target
Making sure the little one doesn't speak
Braided rope slashing thin wrists
He does the disturbing deed
As she begins to cry
He pulls up his zipper
Watching as they run outside
For family dinner

What he did can never
Be forgotten
Will never
By either
Implanting trauma to be selfish
The predator
Remained just that
Nothing more

BLOODLINE

You have blonde hair
I have brown
You've lived a life of acknowledgement
I have always been in denial
You know your descendants
I never met mine
You welcomed me into a home
It will take me awhile
To call it my own

We're not from the same bloodline
I learn my genetics as I age
I didn't have anyone
To compare
Not knowing if we're compatible
Rejected so many times before
I can't trust you just yet
Still engulfed with my abandonment
Maybe this will be the family I accept

MELANIN

Melanin
An evolutionary savior
Protecting against danger
From radiating cancer
A human àdvantage
Biologically gift
Made to increase the survival rate

Melanin
Eyes to hair
Skin seems to be the only care
The suns only competitor
Burning so rare
A defensive privilege
Shades of color

Melanin
Not treated with respect
The word it deserves
Jealousy of such pigmentation
Causing discrimination
With trending proliferation
Now against another cancer

I'M SURE

Both taken by surprise
Friends in a prior life
She spoke to him longer
Going back to his room
Smoking and telling stories
She stared at the tapestry
Telling herself she would not do anything
His hands touched her thighs
That was when she gave it a try

She looked at him straight
Declaring clothes will remain
He said he understood
Still continuing his pursuit
Promises buried with lost trust
With every initiation
She said no to sexual penetration
He asked "are you sure"
She said she was positive
Seven times around

His grip became firmer
Her pleas became louder
She tried to leave
He pinned her down
Body working hard
But embracing gravity
Presenting his uncovered erection

Fighting to remove her underwear
The presence of her fear appeared

Adrenaline raging
Muscles clenched in aggression
Fight surpassing flight
She fought back with every might
Now a battle of strength
She maneuvered with instinct
Until he was off her

She ran faster than ever
He couldn't rape her

NOW I AM

I don't know how I ended up here
Hands red
While my child cries in fear
My spouse screaming without relief
Only aware in my conscious stream

When my fuel gets injected
Drinking my childhood away
The designated imprinted
How to take my own pain away
When other bodies get in the way

Not remembering bare flesh
Without scars and bruises
Benumb to screams
I was mute when abused
And now
I'm the abuser

ALL I EVER KNEW

All I ever knew was how to pull a trigger
Worrying about now while hoping for a later
Meeting my father in jail
Selling addiction to make bail
My mother as my best client
Waiting to be incarcerated

Society did me poor
My skin gave me a code
Poverty taking its strong toll
Shifting my dreams and goals
Family and friends to look after
Titled as the designated provider

It's time
My life be rid of crime
Maybe even an educative dive
Instead of facing prosecution
Earn another reputation

Life and I have not been on the same page
That's up to me to change
Praying to the spiritual
Just hoping it doesn't take a miracle

INSTEAD

6 am, mental haze, unaware
7 am, childcare
8 am, preparation
8 am, sending them to gain education

9 am, you look at them, features so similar
9 am, as they leave you, failure
9 am, kiss them on the forehead
9 am, hoping they gain a different life instead

10 am, staying home
11 am, bills on bills stacking to the dome
12 pm, wipe the grease from the stove
12 pm, barely any food, self-loath

1 pm, eyes closed
1 pm, asleep by accident
1 pm, praying
1 pm, wall starring

2 pm, clean the children's rooms
2 pm, remembering when they were in the womb
3 pm, the children arrive
3 pm, smile so they think you're alive

4 pm, help them with their studies
5 pm, time for work
6 pm, kiss them on the forehead
7 pm, hoping they gain a different life instead

8 pm, start of the shift
8 pm, moral drift
8 pm, preparation
8 pm, no time for hesitation

9 pm, you make your appearance
9 pm, removal of adherence
9 pm, they cheer
9 pm, but it isn't for you my dear

9:30 pm, movement of the joints
9:30 pm, watch as others point
10 pm, slow removal
10 pm, it's getting colder, approval

10 pm, your skin is set free
10 pm, you are surrounded by the leaves of a tree
10 pm, you are called names
10 pm, no one understands the shame

11 pm, it's your turn to shine
11 pm, practiced for this time
11 pm, skin kisses the metal
11 pm, moving as they settle

12 am, it's a continuation
12 am, new outfit, same predictions
12 am, greens held as a stack
12 am, cash so there is no trace back

1 am, circling and circling
1 am, dancing becomes working
1 am, metal becomes a common scent
1 am, cigarettes and beer become translucent

2 am, physical strength to pull up
2 am, in real life it's harder to reach the top
2 am, holding back the tears after a remark
2 am, no emotions, must become dark

3 am, go back home alone to bed
3 am, hanging on by a thread
3 am, kiss the children's forehead
3 am, hoping they gain a different life instead

INVOLUNTARY INDEPENDENCE

She sits in the corner
Waiting to be heard
Attention out of focus
She becomes a blurry object
Proving she's fine on her own
Being separated from home
She learns the world of independence
Never knowing about dependence
She grows to be strong
Reminding herself that everyone
And every relationship is not wrong

He sits in the stands
Waiting to be called
Excitement swims through every bone
Vibration of eagerness
But he seems to be invisible
His reaction, no one notices
So, he learns to be independent
Never having a pack to rely on
Becoming his own best friend
He must learn there are people
He can lean on again

BAIT

At the age of two
The child lies still
Frozen, unable to yell
As the guardian walks in
Picture of protection
The child trembles
Staring into the hallow black eyes
The necessity for separation sprung out
The survival instinct wanted to burst
The habituated knows the routine
The situation could no longer terminate
So, the vulnerable child just waits
Not viewed as human
But as bait

THANKFUL

I'm thankful to have grown up in poverty
Or I wouldn't be as smart as I am currently
Understanding the truth behind the hustle
By way of modesty and always staying humble
Seeing a bigger view
Sacrifice was all that I knew
Falling to learn just how to get through
I did not appreciate before
Though now I do

LAW

What is law
When there are no alterations
Despite reforming generations

What is law
When the people that define it
Decide not to follow it

What is law
When it makes morality unclear
Defining earth as multiple spheres

What is law
When there lacks a consistency
Directing based on feelings personally

What is law
When justice has lost its meaning
Disregarding the lives of other beings

ONLY CHILD

Life as an only child
Terrified that I may have failed
Surrounded by guilt
Foundation left to be built
A path of ambition
To thank the previous generation
Struggle through migration
Now I am the reputation

Life as an only child
Thankful to not have been spoiled
With pressure constantly boiled
Attention becoming torture
The line between rupture
Or success
Being the only common factor
Being all that they have left

SEPARATE

I had to separate
I was begging to forget
My own traits
So, I turned back
And closed the gate

So difficult to do
Like departing from glue
Hating how affected I was
Knowing if it wasn't right
I would lose my own fight

So, I had to separate
To regain what I built
Recollect love and guilt
When drive gave me faults
Secrets cherished in the vaults

Separating
Seemed to be the only answer
Curing myself of cancer
To the health so valuable
I had to leave behind the attachables

ALONE

I've always been alone
Even when I didn't want to be
Guiding my soul
Counseling my own being
Sometimes I hoped someone would come
Arms held wide
They walk towards me
Accepting what is not reality
I don't need it to be
Finding peace in identity
No longer sad
Myself is all I've ever had

COMA

Days passing like hours
Unaware of everything around
Neither future nor present
Incapable of verbalizing
Nothing sensitizing
Deadened in every region
Black is all that's seen
As if time merely froze
Frightened to come out and see
Functional in life
But in a coma inside

FELT AND FEEL

Life
I felt alone
I felt poor
I felt like I had nothing to offer the world
I felt like I wasn't meant for the world
As if reality was a curse
And breathing was its weapon
That life was meant to end
No need to try

I felt like a broken nail
And life was the hammer
Didn't fix anything
Only fell to leave room for another
I felt empty
As if the cup didn't even exist
I felt like a burden
Causing pain to those around
I felt like the world would be better off
If I was just
Dead

I felt like my purpose
Was to die after all
To free the world of a pain
That did nothing at all
Who just took up room
Meant to be brushed away soon
I felt like I couldn't fulfill
What everyone required
That I wasn't the one
That I should be gone

That's what I once felt
That's when I didn't know
What was to finally show
I feel ungrateful by the way I viewed life
Despite
It now being cherished
I once made it a wasteland
Now I can imagine
I feel like I serve a purpose
And there's a reason
I feel like there is a weapon to save the world
Behind my breathing

DISTANCE'S STRENGTH

With miles stretching
Loneliness degrading
Distance creating deprivation
Eyes under sedation
The overlooked factor
Towards intrapersonal recovery
Is comprehending
Distance being just a length
Love is what's indefinite strength

ROAR

Was never thought to love
Defense as the primitive thought
Intuition creating the tough
With words trying to depart
Within its own nurturing walls
An incomprehensible soul
When life mimics each toll
As if what is over
Becomes another item of the hoarder

Trying to move past serenity
Into actualizing reality
Coping actually
But hoping for fantasy
Lost in the visions
Distorted by the truth
Questioning every position
For she was her own supervision

Now moving through the branches
Of breathing plants
She stretches her weakness
To remove the knots within
Voices behind shadows disappear
Watching the roar of strength
Uncover from the suppressed
She relinquishes her distance
She brings life to existence

SAVING ME

Thank you for saving me
When I needed it most
Despite my stubborn mentality
That stopped you from getting close
I didn't think I needed to be saved
Having done so much alone
But because of you
I finally let go

HEALERS

Healers
A granted gift
A divine blessing
With curses hidden inside
So elegant and sly
Chakras aligned
And whispers of serenity
Creating a symbiotic remedy

Despite suffocating traps
The healers don't look back
Their souls intact
Heart reacts
Giving what is necessary
A mental cleanse
With a physical clearance

Meant to reward the lost
With what has been overlooked
Covering the wounds
After removing the smoke
With blood becoming seeds
And tears becoming water
The healers stand together
Letting hope last longer

PRIVILEGE

Everyone possesses privilege
From residing in a location
To the ability to produce creation
The talent behind a voice
The resilience beneath a life of no choice
Excelling in education
Financial rehabilitation
Familiar with love
Surviving when thrown from above
The ability to escape torture
An aesthetically pleasing stature
Surviving dodged bullets
Owning a toilet
The push that led to motivation
The care people forget to mention

Privilege can mean anything
Not just the simple derogatory
It has to do with individual stories
It can be the talent that subsides
The intuition that finds
Fleeing a place of war
Recalling the day before
The ability to use limbs
To know how to swim
The chance to shower
Not allergic to flowers
Comprehending time
A blessing or a crime
Privilege is a word so vague
It's both given and made

FINDING REASONS

Torn between two sides
The one that's wrong
Feeling so right
Doing anything to allow myself to stay
Because it's hard to leave
Creating reasons that are make believe
Influenced by what was originally perceived
Ignoring the negativity
Focused on the sympathy
So much logic saying to depart
Figuring out motives
To not change my heart

Finding reasons to stay
Possibility so off putting
To leave something
That for so long
I was holding

SEXUAL INSTINCTS

Acting to no desire
Of this glorified feeling
This visual tie
Emotional attraction
Spiritual contraction

Different form of energy
Appears in silent circumstances
Becoming sexualized
A captivation
The art of seduction

Acting like there is a repel
From that enticing spell
Hormonal drive
Instinctual thrive
An alluring high

Truth is
Just as in tuned
With what has been missing
The sexual craving
That virginity is hiding

PROMISCUOUS

I'm feeling a bit promiscuous
Come walk into my donjon
Take a sip of this tea
And relax yourself nicely
I'll let my hands intertwine
Like snakes drunk on wine

Release gravity in Zen
Trust the magician
Let yourself fall within
With floating limbs
To the endless tricks
Of the dominatrix

Hoping this isn't a sin
Even so
I'd do it all over again

HER CHOICE

As she sits holding her stomach
Wondering how this could happen
Replaying everything from that hour
Picking herself apart every minute

She sits in disbelief
Forgetting all the goals
She had to achieve
Losing faith in the future to be

Then thinking this was meant to be
She was born to care beyond reasoning
To guide and nurture this being
She saw the smiles that could proceed

Tears surfacing her reflection
She stared until she couldn't any longer
Debating if she was a reason or a statistic
Contemplating the options that existed

She stood holding her stomach
As time comes closer to voice
A childbearing a child
She has made her choice

THE PARADISE OF CONFLICT

They thought it was paradise
That these feelings were normal
Arguing all the time must have meant
Their love was just right
The tones becoming louder
Causing the eyes to vibrate
Like an earthquake
Giving water to the pain
Which must have meant
The relationship was healing okay

Shatters of glass on the floor
Each wanting the other to do more
One thinks they can help the other grow
One thinks and the other doesn't know
Words becoming daggers
Blades getting sharper every day
The poison of each showers
As clarity has lost its way
Something once so perfect
Now damaged in conflict

NOT HIS CHOICE

He swallowed his breath
A final gulp
Recollection of the debates
To be sure of an identity realization
Turning into a societal modification
Preparing for the ridicule
He was about to face

Attraction appearing so cemented
When gravel can be transformed
It isn't the internal acceptance
That brings palpitations so unwarned
Rather the verbal publication
Of how who he loves
Is not considered the norm

If he was given the chance to decide
Within societal parameters he would abide
But the reality is of opposite conversation
Now the choice to live in a lie
Or self-actualization
Expressing love for the same gender
Put him in a difficult position

MANIPULATION

Taunting an intoxication
For love is a drug after all
Feeling addiction as it crawls
Committing to every inch
Of the future duration

Taken under control
Believing everything that's told
Mesmerized by the trusted eyes
Oblivious to the rusted cold
Taken as a captive

So infused in words
Those actions disappear
Slave to the mastermind
The master puppeteer
Manipulating someone dear

LONG TIME

It took me a long time
To accept that people
Don't think like me
They're not driven
By generosity
Not motivated
By curiosity
Not desiring expansion
Comfort is all that's needed

It took me a long time
To accept selfish actions
As a part of human nature
Overcoming my struggles to teach
Pushing people towards
What seems out of reach
Then when the time is right
They cut the ties
Taking advantage of me

HIS SYMPATHY

Living in a life of disassociation
Determined to find determination
To rise above the motivation
That had been lacked in his circle

Enticed by self-redemption
Despite all the belittling confrontations
That led him to the feeling of isolation
So, he began to remove emotion

Not able to grasp certain reactions
How people could desire so much retaliation
Even himself, he began to question
Then he used it as fuel for success

As others saw him as a God like creation
His humble soul created an opposition
He didn't understand the gifts in his possession
Charming with a smile that lures

What was lacking in his nature
He aimed to restore
Still heartbroken from broken relations
His ability for compassion has more power than known

Strength building his stabilization
Tough skin with a mind capable of expansion
He embraced his love and heart with intelligence
Finding the sympathy that was hiding from the storm

SELFLESS

Altruistic by birth
Environment fed into it
Genetics composed it

Giving everything given
Having nothing was fine
If another was alright

Breathing to help the surrounding
Befriending the ones pretending
Stopping lives from ending

Expecting others to be the same
Now aware of the game
People aren't who they claim

Constantly being let down
Continuing to offer all around
Becoming less day by day

A being so selfless
Will only be able to survive
When learning to be selfish

TRAUMATIZING TATTOO

Traumatizing tattoo
Wearing hearts on my sleeves
It's already imprinted on my body
As previous me still grieves
When I wasn't marked permanently
Bare and young skin surrounded me
Before victim to intoxication
Recalling the previous constantly
An open book for interpretations
Self-inflicting morphing
Attention forming
Gone when I close my eyes
No ink showing

Marks forming with mental rigidity
The way skin and air meet
A surface that barriers
The shield to invisibility

Recalling those times
The nightmares called memories
All engraved in every part of me
As soon as I try to forget
My tattoos remind me

I WIN

I want everyone to win
But I'm the winner
No need to argue
I'll confuse you in a circle
Make you think you're right
The will to be so deceitful
You will freeze in shock
But don't worry
I will tell you how to respond

Take these insults
And then come my puppet
There is a reason you're not correct
I will manipulate you like no other
Making you think it was requested
I have every reason to think I'm above
In anyway, I've already won
I see the world flat not like a pessimist
I see it through the eyes of a narcissist

TRUST ISSUES

Trust issues
Formed from the times of misuse
Of abuse
Of being removed
When there was nothing more to do

Trust issues
Formed from fallen expectations
Breaking redesigned foundations
Pretending like the new is different
Though it's just another redundant

Trust issues
They would not have existed
If there was not so much mistreatment
If the same pattern did not continue
Now left with trust issues

LANGUAGE

As they move their mouths
With incomprehensible sounds
Knowing they are trying to voice
Something of importance
Something of relevance

As their hands begin to move
To create diction-based imagery
Trying to draw what they mean
Solely to get me
To begin comprehending

As they are just sounds in my head
Smiling and nodding
Words they know as natural
Leads me to feeling naive
Wishing to understand the native language
As a novel immigrant

FORCED AND ARRANGED

Romance
Was never of importance
It would come when
The time was right
Giving the decision
In the hands of my parents
They sort through options
Finding the perfect match

Marriage
Was always encouraged
With little choice bound
Not much of a concern
There was only so much control
With everything finally set
The wedding came around
The night I first met
Who I would spend
The rest of my life with

WALKED AWAY

I tried to love them
I really did
To look past the mischief
To look past the rebellion
Since it was my fault
I should have raised them
And cared
With more effort and thought
Not let my burden
Become theirs

But I just gave up
Like I did today
Packed up my luggage
One last look
Then never again
Out the door
Then I just walked away

ALIEN

Working to make any change
For food and rent
More hours awake than asleep
But it's worth it for the family
Being given so many
New opportunities
Not even considered as existing
A life of secrecy
If only more aid was provided
No such thing is possible
For the undocumented

NOT STRANGERS

He fell in love
With the woman that birthed him
Jealous of the man that took her
Separated for all his life
He didn't even know them
Strangers at second sight
Instant connection
After weeks they found out
Blood was shared
Never thought to be that category
Just another incest story

DISGRACE

You left
Remains of genetics
That serves no purpose
Stuck in imagination nevertheless
Of why I became fatherless
Never deserved this mess

The meaning of men changed
When the designated protector
Became estranged
Trying to remember how your skin felt
But all I feel is rage
You are your own daughter's disgrace

THE SHELL

Just not ready
To come out of the shell
Take in everything known
Then move forward somehow
Away from a life so comfortable
Conversations not expandable
A life now considered mediocre
The shell was just a protector

The time will come
When the shell will be removed
When thoughts don't have an end
When there is more room
Advancing to the next phase
Becoming mature
Just a little while longer
Until no shell
Means stronger

INFLUENCED

Ready and action
Take the talent
For the financial
Exploitation
With contracts and alterations

As the outside views
Multiple faces on the same body
The original becomes a nobody

With a branded personality
The feature for the future
Boundaries get out of hands
Being followed
Just for breathing in
Everyone ages, everyone grows
Some cases are just seen more

Exceptions granted
Because of the public eye
Influencers that can get by
Even without an alibi
Then becoming a good ally
For the one and a million
That can get through
Prepare for those mental tattoos

Ready and cut
As maturity becomes finding i   dentity
Living a life that isn't normal
It's nice to be influential
Then again, an entire life on air
Not knowing what influence to b   are
Fame contracted through g   ossiping
The spotlight and luxury
Of a celebrity

ACTION

Acting in a move
That's real time
When no one knows
What's playing in the background
An audience of plague
A show of random doubts

Someone saying they're here
Trying to kill me right there
Another saying I'm not worth it
Demeaning my will as a person
There's the entity right beside
Invisible to outside eyes

Not knowing which one to expect
Walking through life restless
Hallucinations of the real
So hard to keep composure
Every dimension is relentlessly frantic
Every show directed by a schizophrenic

FEENING

Looking right back at myself
A face so damaged
I'd try to remember how I was
Used for the advantage of others
Those recalling's are now locked away
No sense in letting them prey
The monster that lurks
The unwelcomed critic

As the water splashes my face
I go to make breakfast
Living on welfare
What keeps my kids fed
A life they do not deserve
Needing to endure
Getting ready to sit down
Then hearing a familiar ring

I kiss my eldest goodbye
It's now up to them
To hold the house down
I walked until my name is called
Preparing for the exchange
Given up my body
For what's in a syringe
One day I promise to change

THE BODY

In one instant
A single screech
The life that was known
Could no longer be
A fight to regain
The crashed identity
A battle of the relentless
And honorary

Handicapped by life's duty
Unable to move freely
Once a simple daily
With vibrating tears
The strongest motion in the body
Frustrating throws
Why would this happen to anybody
Trying to climb with fragile bones

As the days kept passing
The struggle kept harassing
Adjusting to a world
Car crash left defenseless
When the physical and mental
Need to be partners again
It is no longer a fight of survival
It is time for a revival

What was once
Is still beautiful

MISTAKES

It had to be done
Loaded the gun
The door knob
Began to shake
That was the first mistake

Into a hesitant state
Then came the unlock
That was the second mistake

Based on the real
Consequences when deciding to steal
Soon came the third mistake

As the burglar walked in
Owner threatening with a gun
The burglar kept moving along
Showing the carried knife
The invader began to run on
Then came the shot
Silence
Three strikes and gone

NOT WITHOUT ME

It was a mistake
Leaving for that idiot
To live
Everyone craves
Becomes deranged
Deciding to leave
The best person that could be
A beautiful life in front
You left to taunt

Acting on thoughts
Vulgar and violent
A life without me
Can never be greater
It just is not worth it
This was where you belonged
So, let me give you a favor
Rid you of this life for the better
Even if I'm charged with murder

YEARS

It's been a while since they met
One in grade nine
The other in grade ten
Then for some reason
Life caused them to part
Each receiving a fresh start

Fast forward to twelve years down
Running into each other
In their hometown
One already divorced
The other a CEO

They sat down and caught up
About all that time apart
If they are still the same person
If who they were is forgotten
With laughter and tears
The start of the next sixty years

GROOMED

Provided with shelter and care
Saying I love you
Again, and again
A twenty-year age gap
Though nothing seemed bad

Saying words of affirmation
How being in their life is so important
No one loves the way they do
No one else will love you
Being together is for our own good

With years gone by
Never being able to part
Thinking everything was fine
Stuck in Stockholm syndrome
Groomed from middle school and on

FREE

On her sixth birthday
Her father found her a husband
Forty years her senior
He voiced in the name of religion
Interpreting words that were not there
She was thrown to wed a stranger

As she grew into independence
She felt resentment inside
Hating the life, she was forced into
Wanting to run away with another guy
In a county
Where women don't have many rights

As she tried to flee
Her brother came to warn
That if she decided to leave
The family would shun then kill
Able to be imprisoned
For not following the male's orders

She continued to live in agony
Miscarrying every child intentionally
Wondering what was better for her will
She packed up a bag and fled
As soon as she thought she was free
The males abided by the promises

Considered an honorable murder
The father and brother left the body
She was considered property
To listen and obey
Punished through her days
At least now she was free

CONVICTED

When the day finally came
Leaving the metal bars
Entering the real world
Putting resolutions to work
A new person about to start
Placing this one mistake behind
Replenishing the years lost

Walking out into a society
That seemed to excel in time
How much was missed
During the imprisoned crime
Ready to renovate a life and self
Putting everything troubled behind
The real struggle had just begun

Labeled a felon all over the face
Trying to find a steady job and place
But only noted as a wasteful disgrace
The qualification didn't matter
With so many backs turned
Then expected to coexist
So little chances for the convict

SIN

Bound by religion
Suppressed by sins
One wrong glance
Prayers, please forgive
But there's some
Dark secrets
Under the hijab
As so many assume
There is something buried
Strong with faith
But not traditionally wedded
So involuntarily
As if it was innate
This cannot be a sin
In love with another woman

BLANK SLATE

Riches to poor
The immigrants dream
Full of possibilities
Skips a generation
If even achieved

Working tirelessly
All for their offspring's
Giving them a life
Full of greater energy
Greater opportunities

With two degrees each
The parents get ready to leave
To be successful
Having lived a life so educational
Unfortunately, it's not that simple

They begin with learning the language
Then given a blank slate
Everything up to now doesn't count
Remaking a life when middle aged
More expenses and less pay

Adjusting to a new lifestyle
Leveling down from before
Hoping for something
To happen miraculously
Now living like their old employees

As they look into each other eyes
With anger and tears deep inside
They get distracted by the children
Remembering that this was for them
Agreeing they would still to it again

MAN

Getting home late
Another day at the shop
Hard working mechanic
Getting ready for slumber
As he strips down into boxers

Awoken early for the game
Reminiscing about old football days
Then the younger ways
Like he used to in the fraternity stage
Hands slides through his thick facial hair

Wakes up for work
In a nice, collared shirt
Walking towards office
As all the women keep their stare
He smiles a hello their way

Getting home from work
Oil is all over
He strips down
Lays in bed
Next to his husband

CULT GUILT

A light bulb finally hit
Becoming frantic
Realizing boundaries
It was separating reality
Then trying to imprint stories
That could have been made falsely
Only able to believe so much
When the same words show up
The same words the preacher taught

As the heart begins to panic
The head experiences a world wind
Being so far away from open minds
What is truly occurring at these times
Running away to finally escape
Stopped by brain washed acquaintances
Then comes the family and parents
Jumping past their manipulative built
Finally, being free from the cult guilt

REVENGE

All of you bullied me
Telling me I wasn't enough
That I'd never find love
Involuntarily celibate
All the females so ignorant
Not seeing how I'm perfect
I'll show them

Now it's my turn for revenge
For all times I got ignored
Telling me my breathing was a waste
The grave was where I should exist
Not being able to have friends
The weird one, alone to fend
It's not mine, but it's your end

Not expecting what's about to come
Walking into the room of my parents
That never seemed to care
Taking the AK-47
Look, it's time for school
Don't call me a loner
I'm better, the next school shooter

GANGSTER

A strange sight
Tattoos from feet to neck
Not warned by the movies
A danger so extraordinary
With vengeance in eyes
A past internally criminalized
Nothing to lose
No reason to hide
Children to supply
Food to provide

Two pistols always at hand
Ordering the subordinates
To commit what's lawbreaking
Not trying to get caught
The plague of danger
Past the amateur
Not just a regular gang banger
More like an anchor
The life of a real female gangster

PUSH

It was their first child
So excited
They decided to wait it out
For the surprise of their life
The day came for delivery
Fifteen hours gone by already
One push then another
Dilated and ready
Another push then there's the baby

The doctor looks concerned
That the umbilical cord
Was not positioned correctly
But saying the baby will make it
The mother cries as he holds tighter
One more push to birth a soul
As it enters the world
The room gets loud with silence

The parents waiting to hold
What they've been waiting nine months for
They cannot wait any longer
Anticipating a congratulating doctor
As she looks at them in the eyes
With a face so torn
She sincerely says the words
"I'm sorry, it's a still born"
Every heart breaks
The silence has been broken

THERE

They re-adjust the ventilator
Getting ready to feed
Through the thick tube
The parents lift the child
To clean throughout the skin
Holding and modifying
For the third time this morning

Unable to speak
Maybe not even understand
Unable to move
The teenager just stares
While the parent's bicker
About debilitating finances
What life would be like childless

Parents of two
Losing hope and energy for one
Because of genetics
Expected to take care
Of a child hindered to live
All their lives gained weight
Tired but loving endlessly

TRAINED

A mother that would bring home men
Just to abuse all of them
A father that was never around
Siblings learned attack before defense
Feeling tortured and homeless
Left the home before legal
He aged with a mentor

Trained and hooked on drugs
He began to find the vulnerable
That are without a place to go
Wanting protection and stay
So, he offered them what he could
To work with him for a pound of coke
He became their pimp, and they understood

IN PASSING

Found it on the cabinet
Curious as every child is
She took it and consumed it
Then came along her mother
With child molester father
They began to beat her
That's when she first tasted liquor

Her father got arrested
Her mother couldn't handle it
She was raped before knowing sentences
Boyfriend to boyfriend with miscarriages
She left to begin all over again
Without any form of education
Before eighteen she was independent

Now meeting people with promises
Saying improvement is in the processes
She worked as the only thing she knew
That's how she became a prostitute
Began as a minor but it just continued
Beaten by men because they want to
Now hooked on heroin too

She dreams of a day where there's change
Where she can live a life so great
But her mind is deteriorating
Shelter to shelter just not working
Out on the streets since she was a teen
People stared with concern, doing nothing,
She's just another face in passing

DIFFERENT

Born different
Said to have a genetic disorder
Very aesthetically apparent
Trouble with being coherent
No choice but to be a dependent
Being called retarded
Though a person nonetheless

Going through days as much as possible
Difficulties but still capable
Qualities that cannot be controlled
Led to being made fun of and trolled
Smiling everyday like there was no struggle
Enjoying the minutes and hours
Seeing the different as a superpower

WORKING FOR A BREAK

Rehearsing daily
A concert of contests
Fixing the music regularly
As a starving artist

No one believed in them
Creating strength in being solo
Practicing moving the brush smoothly
Writing lyrics that impact accurately

As the sun comes back up
Still working
Going from a minimum wage
To self-support and enough earnings

Putting it out there for the public
Ignored by even friends
Discouraged but never stopping
This is passion that leads to thriving

Knowing there is something special
How it can open and impact people
Be something inspirational
New work keeps coming

Daydreaming now just at night
Tired and restless at the same time
Until finally noticed for goodness' sake
Here comes the awaited break

TIGHTER

She held her baby tighter
So, the crying would get a little quieter
Understanding that the baby
Was probably just overwhelmed
She held tighter so he would calm down

When he had settled
She wished there was day care
Someone to watch him at home
To not bring him on the hour-long train
So, he didn't have to balance with books

She began rocking him
Having to rely on free services
Sleepless nights and finishing assignments
She knew ahead was a beautiful future
Holding him tight she went back to lecture

KILLER

I'm a killer
I'm going to jail
For committing heinous murder
But I feel like the victim here

Parents are supposed to put their child first
Not enable such hate and torture
Not let all this abuse become firmer
I just couldn't handle it any longer

It was never my intention
But the argument suddenly ruptured
Nothing left to lose, already corrupted
My innocence lost and left
All because of selfish them

It just had to end
Finally able to defend
Loaded, clicked and triggered
Parents finally dead

POUNDS

I saw my father die
The day he hit a three hundred pounds
Passing on his genetic obesity

As a child I tried to lower my eating
Disorders pending
I just kept on gaining

Back stabbed by physiology
I became two hundred pounds
Lost the energy to keep trying

Conditions is what killed my father
Something I cannot let happen
Just lost ten more pounds

BYSTANDER

Someone help!
As she remained screaming
Thousands of people
They all kept walking
Could have done something
They preferred to be bystanders

Help me please
But no one turned
That day
Was the first day
Her loved ones mourned

GOLDEN SPOON

Not needing to second think
Always given everything
Fed with a golden spoon
A life of luxurious goods
Financial ease
Choices made as pleased
Since birth and on
Not worrying

There's security in the success
Born to wealthy parents
Until the day it crashed down
Lost every penny in a scam
Familiar just disappeared
A rainfall of crumble
Anxiety that's never been there
About to be dependent on welfare

THE STUDENT

The children put on their backpacks
About to go into natures war
As the parents encourage such conduct
They prepare in groups of three or more

Walking miles in snowstorms
Or excruciating heat
Through rainfalls and thunderstorms
Through any of nature's screams

They walk through obstacles
Using vines and rocks
A path taken most days of the week
To get to school and learn attentively

HIDDEN TORTURE

He was in the eighth grade
A teacher's favorite student
Math was his favorite
Always paying attention
Bombarding with questions

The teacher grew interested in him
She loved what he represented
She loved every way he came off
So, she asked him to stay after class
Offered her number and guidance

They began to text
Not the common teacher-student relation
Then messages became appointments
With hands on interactions
Inappropriate touches

In the day they saw each other in class
The night was a flipped occurrence
They began to engage in intercourse
He felt very violated but not able to voice
He was a boy, he should like the choice

Afraid of the teasing, he kept quite
Lying about where he was going
The home of his deceiving predator
He decided to take it, in silence
Every time his teacher raped him

GYPSIES

They do nothing but beg and steal
Out on the streets, taking other's meals
Unable to get an occupation
Since they all lack motivation
Their homes of dirt just take up room
Deserving to be rid through
No reason to have them in the country
No reason to have those gypsies

I look for work every single day
Fleeing from countries that do not care
Living with a stereotype making us plagues
Not believing in us, no help from government
No opportunities being granted our way
Picking up scraps and trash just to get by
For reasons that are prejudice
Music and tradition keep us going with stride
We are the gypsies, Europe's disregarded

FOSTER

Children being sent off
To foster care and so on
With addicted or abusive parents
Even those that became orphans
They feel misled by the world of no control
Unable to fully grasp, but soon behold
The possibility of being put in a home
Rerunning an abusive cycle
Real but unbelievable

They wanted a family
Able to have their own biologically
But wanted to care for a child
That could be given a second chance
Growing up as normal as possible
They fostered, waiting from hours to years
As the children came and got sent off
Going back to families of the stranded ones
Until the day finally comes
Getting their own little one

PRIVLEDGED GUILT

Mother worked endless nights
To make sure stability was fine
Hustling every day
For her future generations
Slowly from poor to riches
She soared like it was nature
The game of struggle was conquered
Effort is what she taught her family
The children understood the economy
Rooting for everyone trying
Helping anyone in need
But still living with financial guilt

Protesting at every event
Fighting for the minority
Preference towards colored skin
Ashamed by past ancestors
Trying to make amends
For the ones that remain ignorant
Expressing his difference
To be removed from that category
But all people see is white privilege
Though he acknowledges
He still possesses white guilt

He saw his mother get abused
Every day by someone of no use
Refused to ever call him father
Seeing him as inflected poison
Then as he grew older
He began volunteering at women shelters
Looking past their beaten eyes
They stare at him with hesitance
He talks about awareness
When walking them late at night
But it's when he walks alone
That he feels masculine guilt

She was in the driver's seat
Laughing with the other passengers
Singing along to music getting louder
Eyes focused on the road
Then a sudden crash
Harmonizing became screaming
Hit by an intoxicated driver
Crashed, they should not have been there
She fought for dear life
Hoping the other three would be by her side
Then awoken in the hospital
She sustained minor injuries
But the others weren't as lucky
May they Rest in Peace
Living with survivors' guilt

YOUNG TROOPS

Learning how to drive a tank
Handle a rifle and how to shank
Orphaned into a life of war
As just young boys

The orphaned girls become
Just a womb to carry generations on
They had just been planted there
In the countries battle zone affair

Used as the primary defense
Against any external intrusion
The child soldiers are dispersed all around
Battle what raised them after being found

PRIDE

She worked hard
To gain her pride
Achieving the above
But nothing was enough
Toxic screams
Woke her shaking knees
Just by trying to please
The woman that donated
Her genes

As she grew older
She thought it would get better
Introducing a lover
Then a marriage
College education and further
Still the same relation with her mother
She cried to her pillow
Wanting an answer
Pleading to God
Or any Heavenly Father

What the answer was
She knew all along
It was her world
A life her mother did want
Pride was in her own eyes
That was the needed
Everything else was just added

She was the important factor
Who her spirits guided

Deep inside her mother
Experienced the same
But couldn't enunciate
The pride of having a daughter
So strong and brave

GRIEVING

As the eldest of three
She remembers finding her father
Just not breathing
The mother tried everything
But it was too late
Here began the grieving

As a mother of three
With a husband she loved dearly
She woke up next to him
But he was still asleep
Started to panic since he wasn't breathing
Here began the grieving

A father of three
With a bride soon to be
The parents wrapping up their wedding
Excited for the life of glamorous
Then came a car crash that made orphans
Here began the grieving

Parents of three
Loving each one independently
It was one's birthday, so they began playing
Hide and seek until that one went missing
Searching until coming across the body
Here began the grieving

WOMEN

Women with little rights
Around almost every country
As they slowly begin to fight
Only a little are listening
Opening to raise a generation
Of men that understand caring

From the women of Yemen
That fight with the army
To the ones in Sudan
That walk miles for feeding
To the women in Nicaragua
Numb from all the beatings

To all the women around the world
Being sold to wed
To every single little girl
That will lack the recognition they deserve
To every single female
That had their power taken away

The home of humanity
Belittled by their lack of masculinity
But their strength never stopping
With resilience that's never ending
To be a female is anything but fair
People that deserve more care

BOYS

Boys are taught to not cry
Despite any feeling inside
Whether fallen and hindered
Sad and bewildered

Having to be the face of stability
With the only form of masculinity
Accepted in emotional society
Are boys being taught to be angry

Boys are taught to not express
No chance to second guess
Explode instantly
To show assertively

Men are taught to not cry
To love but only sometimes
To not be expressive
Unless its anger

DAYS

3600 days had passed
Until free at last
Tears fell at the retrial
When freeing a criminal
That was wrongly accused
A crime of treason
That just needed a face
To remove commotion
So life could go back into place
As they took another and sacrificed

Fresh air finally hitting breath
Freedom did have a taste
Of satisfaction
The innocent victim
Looks at all the families
Then begins to replay
All the unwarranted days
A sufferer of the system
Now having to readjust
To a life that should have always been

FROM BIRTH

Finally in recovery
After years of suffering
Not because she needed copping
But just pure physiology

Her mother created her path
Before she even had a say
No choice was presented her way
Chemicals running through veins

The umbilical became a needle
The mother became the dealer
And then she was born
With an addiction so clear

JUST ANOTHER DAY

Just another day outside
Playing by themselves
No worries to be found
Then out of no sight
Snatched and taken
From a home and love
Losing a sense of humanity
The child is now alimony

Just another day inside
Trapped in a basement
Treated like a specimen
Wondering if absence is noticed
Waiting to be saved
Picturing loved one's faces
Yet only seeing the tormentor
That took a childhood away

Just another day worrying
As insolation becomes normal
With so much time disappeared
No idea how much is left
A new plan surfaced every day
Waiting for any chance to escape
From a chamber of torture
Ever since being kidnapped

THE LIST

Life with its unexpected events
From healthy to desperate
Time ticking with sweat
Worry becoming transparent
As the organs slowly fade
Illness that takes no mercy
When there's no other option
But to wait as another patient

Slowly accepting death
Meditating to each breath
The pain becomes apparent
Through the eyes of the relevant
Praying for a glimpse of hope
A match with an angel
To no longer just be another name
On the organ transplant list

WORKER

As a virgin
I was put into prostitution
Out of fear of death
A craving for survival

Forced into acts
Not just sexual attraction
It was needed to pass
Another day of respiration

Peers from other countries join
Competition but there's nothing else
Though just a minor
I became a sex worker

MIND TRICKS

You took me at a young age
When I was stagnant and estranged
I trusted you with every whim
Fell in love then life was never the same
You withdrew my feeling of isolation
Abandonment removed from the equation
Then trust became codependence
Trying but I couldn't mend it
We became an explosive corrosion
Without any salvation
You became my temptation
Ruining every ounce of reputation
I thought you were the fix
But I was stuck in my mind tricks

As I look at you, I scream with resentment
My life would have thrived in your absence
I began to pick you up habitually
Waiting to burn you ritually
Smoke you into my bloodstream
Ridding me of my steam
Addicted to you, a chemical
Tolerance indisputable
But I can't go back into that cave
No matter how much I crave
Finally, able to leave your attraction
I spill you in water, discarding addiction
Sixty days sober
A battle of forever

CRADLE

He grabs her hand
Walking in the sand
Love surrounded both
She looked up at him
Waiting for the okay
He nods with a smile
She runs to play

All her life
He's been the only one there
Single since her mother left
To never came back
When she was still so young
She became his everything
And he became hers

With no form of resent
No ounce of regret
This was meant to be
He watches her wonder
Gleaming with laughter
She rushes to him gladly
"Come play daddy"

COVERING

Covering up the face
With elongated arms
Taking hits wherever drawn
Something to lie about later
From bruises to black eyes
Just to drown in toxicity
Love has reached its tolerance
Trying to crawl out of the abuse
Worrying no one will believe the accused
It's his word against hers
And people usually associate
The victim to be the woman
Even when it's the man suffering
Covering his face
As she keeps beating

NOT LIKE HIM

He raised his hand to slap her
Mid way in air
He stopped himself against instincts
With drugs in his system
Rage in waves of tsunamis
Becoming the very thing he resented
Like his father that was never present

Remorseful for his actions
He begged for forgiveness
Promised it would never happen
For the millionth time
She no longer believed him
Hated himself for being like his father
In recovery to never become him

TURNED OUT DIFFERENT

He turned out different
From a drug driven father
An overdose survivor
A mother so passive
Insecurity controlled get life

He grew up around gangs
Every week and new illegal plan
In a pattern of selling drugs
He accepted
But never participated

He used his life circumstances
Wanting to be the exception
Hustled through legal success
An influential representation
He turned out different

MENTAL ILLNESS

Maybe mental illness is a superpower
Such a taboo because not everyone has them
Some turn into villains like in every story
Some into heroes with glory
Embracing it at different spectrums
But able to see and feel things special
Something magical
Others cannot even comprehend
What's going on inside the head

It can be overpowering
Or just enough
Learning how to control
Letting it take control
Practicing the sport
Becoming successful
One with the spiritual
Impactful of some kind
Maybe the mentally ill
Are the gifted minds

CAUGHT ME

Lost my way for a minute
Then life became apparent
I met the love of my life
Telling me what I've been missing
For all this time
Knowing everything I didn't even
He showed the real world

We got married quickly
I changed my religion willingly
Supporting him in every cause
Even when others degraded his faith
Though praying to the same God
They tried persuading me he was wrong
But I'll pick my husband over anyone

I became pregnant
He would risk his life in violence
Just to prove nothing at all
Claiming it's for the better
All the explosions and kills
Have logistical causes as well
To just trust him

Pregnant for the third time
Now he's never home
In love with his weapons
Evil becomes his eye color
He assured me it's fine
He's providing security
For our children and mine

The news station was doing a report
On a group of people that revolt
How many lives had been demolished?
Some just so tragic
Exploding morgues created
Something all too familiar

My husbands on the screen
In handcuffs, embarrassingly
I had encouraged that way of living
Now I'm being labeled as guilty
Putting me in a prisoner's camp
With terrorists forging to be Islamic
Now I'm known as the wife of ISIS

BLISSFUL IGNORANCE

First time at the beach
The children run on three
Letting go of hands
Chasing along the sand
Touching the oceans waves
Like it's a new discovery
For everyone there

With eyes and mouth open wide
Excitement swirls around
The toddlers scream and shout
A new exciting part to existence
As they too are a wave of innocence
A stream of consciousness
The tide of blissful ignorance

FINDING

They tell me I'm beautiful
Attracting every being
That my body is majestic
Perfect curves
And whatever there is
They call me a model
Some more subtle
Perfect picture presented

If I am that description
Why do feel such rejection
Seeing a hideous nature
In my eyes I am
Someone no one wants to be
Despite the words of affirmation
People think I'm confident
I wish that was it

Complimenting my appearance
As if there was nothing more
I just hate myself from the core
Still unable to confine
In the person I don't know
But calling myself
I appear different to the majority
Honestly, I'm still finding me

STREETS

Raped at the age of five
Pushed from home to home
Another abuse here
Taken advantage of there
Her life was already chosen
Before she understood choices

I'M SORRY

I'm sorry you had to go through that
I hope now you see yourself
As the beautiful individual you are
Sometimes life is hard like that
Telling yourself you're just enough
Looking in the mirror
Then sweating with fear
Looking at every meal
Like it all ends here

I'm sorry you had to go through that
It must have been so tough
Counting the calories
But still purging away
Or just not eating that day
As anxiety tears you inside
That you just don't look right
Then compliments make their way
Reaffirming why it's okay

I'm sorry you had to go through that
All that constant thought
Worries revolving in the same spot
Even when you say it's ridiculous
It'll come back with vengeance
Maybe this will be the last time
You're beautiful, you must know that
You're able to get past this hell
If I did it then you can as well

THE WALKING JOURNEY

One step, two steps then three
Without any currency
In their native country
They begin their new journey
Walking thousands of miles and miles
To another residency
Just to be able to afford breathing

As they walk through the rocks and dirt
Holding the family that seem weak and sick
Their journey can't stop there
They either make it or end up dead
Walking four days straight
Little sleep and even less to eat

The migrants walk from Africa to Middle East
At the sea for approval to go across
Depending on smugglers and the holy cross
Knowing all the struggle there is to await
They pack up resilience and faith
Risking their lives and burying others
Just to find a job and be a provider

One step, two steps, three
Walking away from a life of poverty
Even if its towards war, even if it repeats
It's better than what they used to see
A journey of four weeks
Kept pushing until they couldn't
With scars and bruises they move forward

PLEASE GOD

Please God
Give me a sign
Give me an answer
On not just a direction
But a reason
The indentation
The message

Please God
Give me a lesson
With a conclusion
That forms a path
To let a change last
A start to be different
A voice to be stronger

Please God
Give me a chance
A coin and a well
To no longer dwell
Surrounded with care
Obtain a wonderful tale

Please God
Listen to my prayers
As I don't as for much
I just ask for you to share
Your advice of the truth
Honest and allude

Please God,
I'm in need of your help
I don't know where else
If not an epiphany
Then some form of clarity
I come here and ask of you
to give me some sort of clue

Please God,
I no longer know what to do

IN LOVE

I'm in dismay
I was trying to go every other way
Get this concept isolated
From every conclusion created
But it wasn't strong enough
So, devastating
A tragedy of the new era
How many moments
Now become what could of's

I just can't continue any longer
The way we see each other
Are the highlights of opposites
Two different extremities
Now there's only one destination
Opposing desires to tear apart
Will never be like the start
I guess this is the end
Why did we have to fall in love with each other?

HOME

Not knowing where to sleep later
The need for courage
A vehicle made to be a savior
As a home and storage
Battle of the fittest behaviors
While on the next voyage

Every night a worry
Moving from scene to scene
Having themselves only
Trying to remain clean
Praying for every day clearly
Living by being a fiend

Another body on the streets
Looked past it as if delirious
Finding anything to eat
In this passage so rigorous
The suns a reminder of repeats
The site of being homeless

JUST WORK

Another day at work
Months down the road
A couple more left
Until he can go home

Hours of driving across
Risking lives every instant
With valuables of high costs
Staying away through the distant

Anticipating his family to hold
Having to pull over just for the needs
Accustomed to sleep being controlled
Just so he can feed

Excessive hours awake
Just to get through faster
Putting everything at stake
The life of a truck driver

SWITCHED

I called you dad for eighteen years
Then a part of you disappeared
Making a new life appear
Another version of you
But this time the hidden honesty
Defying nature and society

I'm proud of you
For becoming who you want to be
But it did distort me
You randomly switched
Going from pants to a skirt
I don't know what to call you anymore

I DO

I solemnly do
Forever and beyond
Take you as my partner
Love you as my will
My start to a family
To be together for eternity

I solemnly do
Forever and beyond
Take you as my partner
Love you as my will
My start to a family
To be together for eternity

I solemnly do
Forever and beyond
Take you as my partner
Love you as my will
My start to a family
To be together for eternity

The three hold hands
As the ceremony gets closer
To almost being over
Rings crossing over
The night of their wedding
Finalizing polygamy

SPIRIT

To bring ease and comfort
Birth spiritual discovers
Belief in something of power
Believing there's something higher
Beholding what is to be gained
Something looking after me
Lessons to keep praying
There always lies a possibility
The creation of a community
The future of a better me
Relining my doubts
To make it seem fine
God helped my life

Just that little of faith
Makes wonders escalate
A connection so divine
Just feels so right
To create a reason
For something outrageous
Even if it's not religious
It's the spirituality that captures
Making sense out of
The reason this world matters
Behind why things happen
Spirituality a relief of comfort

RELIGION

Creating advise without context
Like Christ told them himself
Everyone is just
Interpretations
From a book on a shelf
Based on what they were previously told
Killing childhood
When it did not have to

As word of mouth carries through
But if no one knows the definite truth
Then who's lying and who knew?

Religion creates brainwashed beings
Teachings beginning
To babies not speaking
Molding reasons to leave reality
Pretending everyone is good hearted
And destruction does not exist
The good religion carries
Can disintegrate easily

If you fast and pray
Wear a symbol of faith
Then you'll be okay
The reality is
Life doesn't work that way

Forming more exclusion than unity
Images people pretend to be
While still discriminating
As if God had time to watch everybody
It is just another fairy tale
One which has a hell

Forced into something open-ended
Said to create the open-minded
But it just gets claustrophobic
Every story having an objective
The words on a scripture
Become the rules so closed-ended

No reason to believe in imaginary
Religion is just disappointing

THAT IS WHY

What was, just isn't there
Love became zero care
Two complete opposites
Forced together by an accident
Now having to spend the
Rest of our lives
Mutually trying to get along
Not happy and no energy
That is why, I cheated

It wasn't accepted at the time
Going along with society
It's reproductive pressures
All done and married
But something was always missing
The love soon became apparent
Attraction not being there
Was always truly gay
That is why, I cheated

Tried to get out multiple times
Always a new plan next in line
The term separation
Never registered in their head
Thinking our love was forever
When it was clearly dead
Threatened so I couldn't leave
Efforts to escape unweave
That is why, I cheated

They did it first
So, it was only right
For me to do it back
A motive for revenge
Made from a desire for romance
A redemption of strength
Just so I could feel again
The power to cause the same pain
That is why, I cheated

DO YOU KNOW CHEATING?

Do you know what cheating does?
It doesn't just break a heart
It changes a view
A perspective and how to see new
Trust issues
Questions for every question
How a reality so cherished
Could become so altered
Visible became reshaped
Self-esteem in rage
Help doesn't scream
Addicted to routine

Do you know what cheating does?
It tears another apart
Hyperventilating
Without over reacting
Try to relocate self-identity
When the one that protected you
Is who pulled the trigger on you
It creates an illusion
Seeing people with new perceptions
A deception with intention
Now multiple worlds crumble
All because of a selfish trouble

You will revive from this poison
There's only one thing to do
Appreciate the individual you

IDENTICAL TWIN

Identical twin boys
Separated so young
One went with their dad
And the other with mom
Raised in two neighborhoods
Miles apart
Yet considered enemies
In the street's directory

The twins grew
Then fell into the same shoes
Gangs considered a culture
At the age of nine
Both knew how to shoot a gun
They had still never met
But knew the other existed

Protecting their hoods
No matter what that means
The twins, on opposite teams
For the thrill of the game
People, as targets to eliminate
Gang became family after all
Brothers till the end of all

Before their eighteenth birthday
They each were awarded
A chance to move up in rank
Both needed to do one last errand
Handed a name on a paper
Time to get away with murder
They went to find their victim

They each see the color
Representing the rival
Loading their guns with ammo
By chance, both had the same quest
One quick kill then forever respect
Seconds before they go into attack
They see their own face looking back

EYELIDS

My grandmother shook her head
When she found my mom half dead
Overdosed so nonchalantly
Breathing partially
Then laughing hysterically
My mother was dying

Everything froze
Except my grandmother's voice
Praying to the clouds
While screaming where to be found
Shivers ran behind each breath
As I stared at my mom's eyelids

GRANDPARENTS

Another night of cops at the door
The same reason they always come for
Updating the grandmother regretfully
Her child got caught for drugs and burglary
She knows and acknowledges
Thanks, the officers and turns around
Her grandchildren anticipating their parents
But becoming less hopeful
Then barely even caring anymore
Every night becomes more comfortable
The grandparents took on both roles

I grew up as the eldest of four
My first friends were the cops at the door
Knew my family by name
Their visits were a reminder
That my parents had made another mistake
Locked up to be taken away
My grandmother turned to distract me
But I no longer felt anything
Soon our parents became
The ones who raised us from the beginning

LIVES MATTER

Black lives matter
Brown lives matter
Red lives matter
Yellow lives matter
Orange lives matter
White lives matter

Assigning color to identities
Categorizing importance
Then making the world potent
While defending people
Based on something
Without representation

Assigning lives to colors
To make it easier
If lives matter
Then why are there killings
Based on colors

CHILDHOOD

Take me to childhood
When sins aren't understood
Imaginary friends are what I could use
To resolve my emotional confused

Take me back to when
I could just play pretend
That's how we would escape
Through healthy ways

Take me back to times so influenced
Imprinting for the future
Setting up my traumas to broadcast
The moments of innocent laughs

Take me back to my childhood
Where it was okay to be ignorant
Bliss and all its components
Where bad is not without good

RELATIVE

Every life is relative
Which is why it can't compare
To that of another figure
The hidden drive to be different

Whether
Hollywood fame
To an average abundance
Or struggling for resources
Every person still has something
Affecting them

One's problems shouldn't be disregarded
Since it didn't start as low like another
When patterns alter
From what they're used to
It can influence
In similar ways
A relative world of contraries

REFLECTION OF TIME

We are all a reflection of time
Personality transforming
Children of vulnerability
Wrinkles appearing as days go on
Death at any moment
Age reaching peak
Before deteriorating

No matter the background story
Or social category
Time goes on for everyone
Reflecting a fluid identity
With the same entrance
And exit
We are all just a reflection of time

IMPACT

Be
An impact
Do not settle back
That won't last
Evidence is effect
Engagement is the subject
The influence upholds
If passion
Isn't let go
Impact

THANK YOU

Please be kind to one another, you never know what
someone is going through. Everyone is of
importance. At the end of the day, we are all human
and anyone can make an impact.

The proceeds of this book will be going to:

UNICEF

UNICEF is a charity that works in over 190 different countries in order to provide essentials to disadvantaged children. These children include those in poverty, undergoing a health crisis, refugees, and other vulnerable groups. Their services include health care and immunizations, safe water and sanitation, nutrition, education, emergency relief, pregnancy with birthing aid, as well as receiving a legal identity.

UNICEF helps children live a childhood, which is something everyone deserves.

You can make your own personal donation at:
https://www.unicef.org/
https://www.unicefusa.org/
https://www.unicef.ca/en
https://www.unicef.org.uk/
https://www.unicef.org.au/
Any UNICEF website based on your country.

The goal of each book is to help people, whether with words, finances or any other acts of services.

OTHER BOOKS:

Reality's Dreams

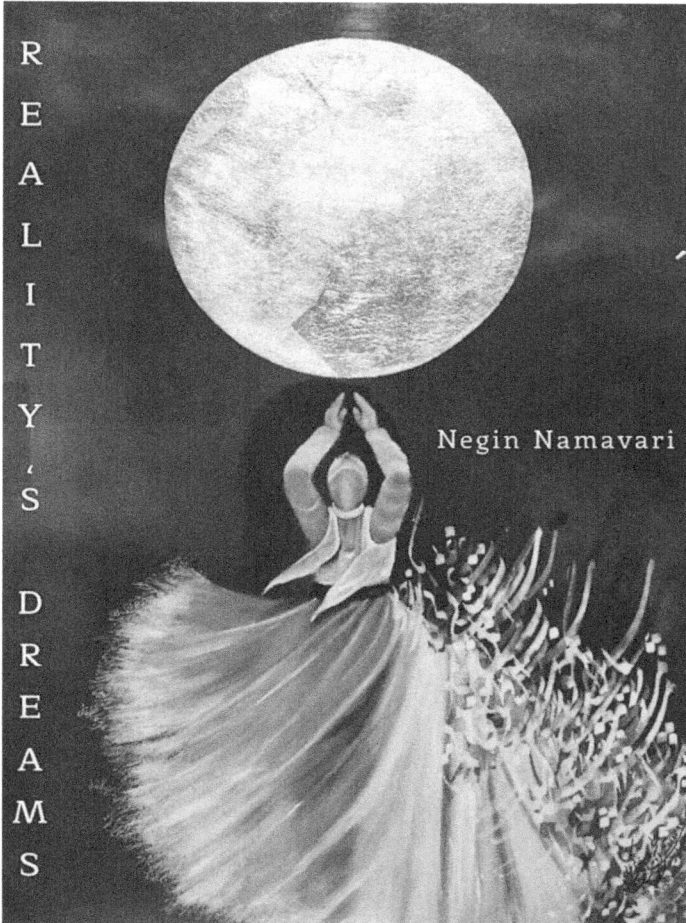

Made in the USA
Las Vegas, NV
07 January 2025

16000169R00085